MW00940825

The White Box Club
HANDBOOK

Simple Tools For Career Transition

Michael Thomas Sunnarborg

The White Box Club Handbook:
Simple Tools For Career Transition

Edited by Kellie M. Hultgren & Elizabeth (Bette) Frick, PhD, ELS
Cover design by Scott Smith, 12 50 Design, Asheville, NC
Interior design & layout by Kiernon James
Back cover photo by Richard Yates
Printed by CreateSpace
Distributed by Creative Consulting

Find links to this book online at:
michaelsunnarborg.com/books

ISBN-13: 978-1515051787
ISBN-10: 1515051781

10 9 8 7 6 5 4 3 2 1

For my Peggy.

Dedicated to all White Box Club members,
whoever and wherever you are. Keep the faith.

PREFACE

Here's the deal. This past spring, I had a moment of truth. You know, one of those moments where your entire life comes to a complete stop and you are suddenly staring at yourself in the mirror, asking the question, "Now what?"

After publishing a series of books about finding better balance in life, I was working on a manuscript for my next book. And although writing and speaking are my passions, working a full-time job keeps gas in my tank and food on my table. These are just the realities of life.

Then one morning, without any notice, I was told that my full-time job was over. I couldn't believe it. I loved my job and the people I worked with each day. I wasn't prepared to leave it so suddenly. I never thought this would happen to me.

I decided to use this experience as a learning opportunity. Just as the proverbial phrase suggests, "When life hands you lemons, make lemonade." This book is the lemonade.

I hope that the personal observations, insights, and stories I've used to help me get through this challenging, yet powerful, experience will help you navigate through your career transition. Sometimes the only way to truly learn from something is to fully experience it. This book can help you to embrace the events of your life, ride the waves of change, and come out better for it in the end.

Life goes on!

Michael Thomas Sunnarborg
September 2015

INTRODUCTION

A layoff or career transition is a major life event. It's a big deal for anyone.

Sometimes during major life events, we want to hurry up and get through the discomfort without taking time to respond thoughtfully and deliberately to the situation. A sudden career transition is a good example of this. If we are triggered into fear, our first response might be to frantically rush out and take any job—anything to keep our income flowing and our lifestyle uninterrupted. Or, we can choose a different response.

This book is about walking down that different path.

In the following pages we will be discussing how to respond to sudden career transitions in gentle, self-aware, and thoughtful ways so that the next step on your career path is a positive one. Doesn't that feel like a more mature and mindful approach?

You have the potential to experience a healthy career transition no matter where you are on your journey, but in order to move through something, you first need to accept it. Sometimes acceptance doesn't come easily—it takes courage, dedication, and commitment. Integration comes in small steps. By seeking to understand yourself better, learning to focus your energy, and practicing new healthy habits, you can get through anything, especially something as challenging as a career transition.

There are three parts to this book, each focusing on one of three stages of awareness, alignment, and activation. Each chapter explores an aspect of the career transition process, primarily focused on how to survive and bounce back after a layoff. Each chapter has been written to gently shift your perspective and provide you with helpful tools and exercises to assist you.

At the end of each chapter are bulleted summary points called a *Reality Check,* along with questions to ponder. You might find it useful to journal about the questions or simply mull them over during your day. They can also serve as a useful meditation focus. Simply bring the questions into your mind during your regular meditation practice and notice the thoughts that float up in response.

I've also added *Inner Affirmations*—positive messages for you to consider as you process the content from each chapter. These messages are coming from my inner voice, or "Wise Will," and are the guiding thoughts that helped me get through this challenging life event. My hope is that they will help and guide you as well.

A few of the chapters have a Supplemental Exercise located in the back of the book. These exercises include helpful checklists or templates designed to enhance the chapter content.

One final note: The chapters address the process of career transition chronologically and will make the most sense if read in order—at least the first time through. Then after you've completed the book, you can return to any of the chapters or exercises to refresh yourself as needed.

A career transition, like any other major life event, can be a poignant and cathartic experience. It can also be a powerful opportunity to learn more about yourself and the world around you. It all depends on how you see it. Join me on this journey as I introduce some simple tools for career transition.

PART I:
AWARENESS

Now What?

CHAPTER 1 — THE ANNOUNCEMENT

*Don't be afraid of change, because it is
leading you to a new beginning.*
— Joyce Meyers

My day started like any other Friday. I got into the office, unpacked my things, and started to prepare for the day. As I checked email, I noticed that an "urgent meeting" had been added on my calendar for 9:00 a.m. that morning. I thought to myself, *this must be about the new product changes. Great!* So at 9:00 a.m., I went to the conference room, took a seat, and waited patiently. At 9:05 a.m., our CEO quickly entered the room and closed the door behind him.

"I've called you together this morning to make an important announcement. We're taking a new direction with the company and all of you in this room are not included. You are being let go immediately. You will be given a severance package including any unused vacation, and HR will be contacting you to follow-up. There are boxes out front for you to take back to your desks, pack up your things, and leave the premises within the hour. We are sorry to do this, but it was a necessary step."

Announcements like this are not uncommon. Not anymore. While in the past our chances of being laid off from a job may have been rare, the speed of today's business and the exponential acceleration of technology have caused our world to change size and direction more rapidly than ever before. As companies react to these changes, they grow in some areas and shrink in others. And while many companies work hard to keep good talent, the odds are good that at some point, you'll be part of a group that no longer has a place in the business plan.

> Midway through the announcement I started to think. *Wait a minute. This can't include me. This is about the other employees. I must have been invited to this meeting to help facilitate the process. Seriously, I just got a raise last month; I'm developing a whole new program for a new product; and I've been told how fantastic my work is, so this is obviously some sort of mistake. Right...?*

> No. I was included, along with a room full of others. In less than 60 seconds it was over. We slowly rose from our chairs and left the room. No one spoke a word—there was only awkward silence.

> What just happened?

Layoffs have been around since the beginning of employment, but in the rapidly changing landscape of our current business economy, they seem to be more common. Any worker could be laid off: corporate executive, janitor, teacher, or sales clerk. No one is immune to business restructuring.

First reactions to being laid off are usually, "Why me? What did I do wrong?" We may automatically assume we are to blame for this unexpected change when, in reality, the layoff had nothing to do with us, personally. Layoffs are business decisions based on restructuring and realignment for business reasons and generally not based on personal performance. However, just because it is a business decision doesn't mean it doesn't *feel* personal. We are all human beings with feelings, so how can we *not* take something like this personally?

> I was numb. I stopped at the front desk, picked up a white box and carried it to my desk. I looked around my office at everything I'd created over the last two and a half years, and suddenly realized it was no longer mine. Some people came over to hug me. I felt like I was dreaming. The whole situation felt surreal. It took everything in me just to stop, breathe, and start gathering up my things.

> I had just become the newest member of **The White Box Club**.

When we experience an intense moment or receive unexpected news, our tendency is to hold our breath. Holding the breath lets us experience a feeling of being in control—at least for the moment. But we eventually must exhale. Consciously breathing out can create a feeling of release. The act of exhaling allows us to relax and let go. Although breathing consciously is temporary, it can bring a bit of relief. Sometimes, breathing is all we can do.

In the moment of a layoff, it's virtually impossible to think. It's hard to remember that you have become wiser, larger, and more powerful than you were before this job. In the words of a former colleague, "You can lay off an employee, but you can't lay off their experience." Looking back on this in the future will remind you that it was a big event—a life-changing moment—and like all other major life events, **this too shall pass**.

REALITY CHECK

- If you've been laid off, it's not about you.
- You've done nothing wrong.
- Layoffs are a business decision.

QUESTIONS TO CONSIDER

1) How can I support myself during this difficult time?

2) How can I learn to accept this even though I can't control it?

INNER AFFIRMATIONS

"I don't need to figure out what's going to happen next for me right away. In due time I will find new direction, but for now I'm going to take time to step back, process, and reflect. Tomorrow is another day and another opportunity to recreate myself again.

In the meantime, I just need to breathe."

CHAPTER 2 — WHITE BOXES

Start where you stand, and work with
whatever tools you may have at your command,
and better tools will be found as you go along.
— George Herbert

Transitions are a part of life. But sudden transitions, especially when they come by surprise, can be shocking and traumatic. An unexpected layoff is such an event.

When a layoff transition is gradual, so is the consolidation process. But in a "white box" layoff, there isn't time to sort and prioritize. The thought of sifting through months or years' worth of materials and files in an hour seems preposterous. An immediate layoff isn't about giving anyone time to organize and transition. It's a clean break, a quick cut—and it slices through all company connections instantly: relationships, intellectual ties, and personal investment in the work are severed.

We all have *white box moments*: events that take us by surprise and force us to be present while not knowing what will happen next, leaving us stunned and utterly speechless.

We walk away from those moments with *white boxes*: containers that hold valuable personal property from past jobs, relationships, or other cathartic experiences. Although these boxes might be physical cartons filled with material objects, they're also containers filled with intangible things. White boxes are packed with memories and emotional triggers. And despite their powerful significance, they often stay packed away in basement storage rooms or back closets only to face their fate in a garbage can or dumpster in the foreseeable future.

Although white boxes contain evidence of endings, they also hold memories of new beginnings. White boxes contain powerful personal history. Sometimes those pockets of memories remind us of who we were and who we've become. They become the map tacks along our career path.

> Within 20 minutes, I had finished packing my white box with the few items that belonged to me, grabbed my coat, and headed out the front door. And just like that, my career with the company was over: a grand total of 35 minutes from announcement to exit. My job had disappeared. And so had I.
>
> I went out to my car, put my box in the trunk, and sat in the parking lot attempting to process what had just happened. I was stunned. My brain was trying to come up with a plan, but to no avail.
>
> After about ten minutes, I drove home, placed my white box on the kitchen counter, sunk into the couch and stared blankly at the wall in silence. It was 10:00 a.m. on a Friday morning, but if you'd asked me what day or time it was, I couldn't have told you.
>
> Besides the immediate shock, what I felt most at that moment was profound sadness. I just left a job I really

loved, and the people—both coworkers and customers—who came with it. I didn't get to finish a project I'd been working on for months. I didn't get to say goodbye to more than a handful of coworkers. I didn't get to notify any of my customers. **I didn't get any closure**. And now I was left to sort it out for myself.

Then the thoughts returned. *Why me? What did I do wrong? This wasn't supposed to happen to me. I coach people about how to deal with losing their job. I'm not supposed to be going through it myself!*

Then the reality returned. It did happen. It was me. I did nothing wrong. And now it was time for me to surrender to this experience.

REALITY CHECK

- Life consists of beginnings and endings.
- We all have white box moments and memories.
- Sometimes the best thing we can do is to simply acknowledge our feelings.

QUESTIONS TO CONSIDER

1) In what ways have other white box moments affected my life? How have they changed things for the better?

2) What are some of the emotions I've experienced during major life changes?

INNER AFFIRMATIONS

"Even though this experience feels surreal right now, I will acknowledge my feelings and not think too far ahead. I have always grown from conflict, and this can be an opportunity for positive change. I only need to believe that everything will be okay and that I can take one moment at a time."

CHAPTER 3 — MONEY MATTERS

The amount of money that a person has in his bank
account is not determined by his starting capital but by his
knowledge about money and his ability to manage it properly.
— Sunday Adelaja

A sudden layoff or job transition can be one of the most devastating experiences to happen to anyone; however, it can also be an opportunity to take advantage of the many support systems specifically put in place to help people through such transitions. City, state, and federal governments have created programs to provide financial and emotional support to people in need. Being in transition puts you directly in a position to receive benefits from these programs.

Whether you've been unexpectedly laid off or left your present employment for another reason, a task of utmost importance is to assess your current financial situation. It is imperative to do this as soon as possible, as your income flow will be changing dramatically.

Taking time to undertake financial assessment includes reviewing:

- **Automatic payments:** monthly bills, expenses, mortgages, car payments, etc.
- **Lifestyle amenities:** household services, memberships, subscriptions, etc.
- **Payments to financial accounts:** 401K, IRA, ROTH or other accounts

For more details about how to organize your finances, see the *Appendix A: Financial Assessment Checklist.*

In a layoff situation, unemployment insurance can provide a critical benefit for keeping a steady stream of income flowing. Unemployment programs are governed by the laws of your state and have slightly different guidelines depending on the region in which you live. Eligibility for unemployment is based on several factors including your previous salary, length of employment, amount and duration of severance (if any), among other variables.

By initiating the unemployment application process, you will receive information indicating what type of unemployment insurance you qualify for, the amount of weekly benefit, and the length for which you can request benefit dollars. With the rapid integration of technology, most unemployment applications and funding requests now can be filed online or by phone.

In addition, you may also be eligible for federal financial assistance programs such as the Dislocated Worker program, which provides support to those considered "permanently" laid off—meaning they are unlikely to return to their previous industry or occupation. Be sure to check with your local employment centers regarding your eligibility status. Re-employment counselors and other support staff can assist you with determining the benefits available in your state and region. More benefits are covered in Chapter 13.

Within his first month of being laid off, Jason was required to attend a re-employment workshop at a local WorkForce Center. He initially thought that the session would be boring and unnecessary, but as it was a mandatory step for receiving unemployment insurance, he needed to attend.

Within the first fifteen minutes after the workshop started, however, Jason was glad that he had shown up. One of the first things he learned was the importance of managing money and how to assess his current financial situation. The workshop facilitator outlined a simple process using a spreadsheet that would help anyone to organize and prioritize his or her financial accounts and obligations. Even though Jason considered himself savvy about money matters, this simple approach to organizing his accounts made sense.

When he got home, Jason put together his own spreadsheet containing his outstanding bills, investment accounts, and other financial information. He found that having all of his financial data in one report gave him a better picture of his financial position. Not only did this provide him with a place to keep his cash flow organized, it also gave him one less thing to think about. This gave Jason the best thing of all: peace of mind.

REALITY CHECK

- Transition time is a good opportunity to organize your finances.
- Help and support are available. You don't need to figure it out on your own.
- There are financial resources and benefits for you. As a taxpayer, you have contributed to these programs!

QUESTIONS TO CONSIDER

1) How can organizing my finances help ease my mind during my job transition?

2) How can being more open to help and support benefit me during this time?

INNER AFFIRMATIONS

"There is an abundance of help and support available to me at all times. I have direct financial benefits available to me, and I have only to learn how to optimize their use. I have the ability to organize and control my financial needs."

Chapter 4 — The Empty Inbox

The answer to every adversity lies in
courageously moving forward with faith.
— Edward Mbiaka

When you experience a significant event in your life, your first reaction may be to tell someone. And with the advent of social networking, some people broadcast their stories like a 24-hour news channel. Individual life events are more public than ever before, and with this potentially larger exposure, the number of people who can respond to our stories is even greater.

Telling our white box stories will bring a wide variety of responses from others, most of which will be based on each individual's experience with job loss or another similar life event. Some responses will be helpful, while others may just express concern or support. Some people won't respond, perhaps because they don't know what to say or the subject may hit too close to home. Either way, it's nice to know that other people are aware of what we're going through. Expressing our feelings out loud, especially to someone else, can bring a sense of relief. There is power in proclamation.

For people who aren't familiar with the growing trends toward business restructuring, there might be an initial shame or a stigma associated with being laid off. However, today's business market is more agile and flexible than in the past. Being laid off is becoming more common, so **we don't need to be afraid to tell our stories**.

> At first Kyle wasn't sure if he wanted to tell anyone besides his family that he'd been laid off. But after some thought, he realized that his friends and family have always been supportive of him no matter what the circumstance, so why should this be any different?
>
> Kyle wasn't accustomed to asking for help, but this was one of those moments where he wanted to reach out and allow others to support him. He decided to post a note online as well as send out short emails and text messages to selected friends.
>
> For the next two weeks, Kyle found himself wading through waves of phone calls, text messages, and emails from friends and family expressing their love and support. People he didn't even know were sending messages of hope and encouragement through social media outlets. The outpouring was amazing.
>
> Then, exactly two weeks after the shocking event, his inbox was almost empty—hardly an email, phone call, or text message related to the layoff. It suddenly felt like the whole event had never occurred. But it had.
>
> So what was this all about?

Even when life slams on the brakes for you, the rest of the world keeps going. Every life event has a process—a beginning and an end—and so do the people touched by it. When others near us are swept into the emotional waves of a personal life event, they, too, become a part of it…for a short time. But then they return to their own lives. They come, they love, and they leave. And life continues.

> As he thought more about it, Kyle realized that the responses from others had simply run their course. And even though he could understand the concept, he still couldn't help but think to himself, *so if other people can move on so quickly, why can't I? How come I can't just process the sadness and disappointment and get over it? Because it happened to me.*

People who are not directly impacted by an event can process faster because **sympathy can only take us so far**.

Even when we extend support to others, we have an intrinsic need to nurture ourselves; when something happens to you, your own process will always be different from anyone else's reaction to that event. Each of us integrates life changes in our own way and in our own time. Being aware of this will help us to honor the unique process for everyone, including ourselves.

REALITY CHECK

- Nobody understands a situation like the person who is in it.
- While others may no longer react to an event the way you are reacting, they may still feel connected to you.
- Don't be afraid to ask for help when you need it.

QUESTIONS TO CONSIDER

1) Whom have I told about my layoff or job transition? Why some and not others?

2) How am I allowing others to help and support me when I need it?

INNER AFFIRMATIONS

"I know that this time of great change will bring about many new experiences, feelings, and responses from others. I also know that many of the challenges are temporary, and I am willing to be open to the support and encouragement that I will receive from others."

CHAPTER 5 — THE POWER OF GRIEVING

With the new day comes new strength and new thoughts.
— Eleanor Roosevelt

Grieving is a natural emotional process that every one of us experiences in one form or another throughout our lifetime. There are many theories about why and how we grieve, and while the process of grieving is most often associated with death, we can still feel intense distress over any kind of loss, including a job loss.

So you might tell others, "Oh it's just a job. It's not like somebody died." But we know it's more than that. For most of us, work is a significant portion of daily life, and for many, has helped them to define their purpose and direction. Losing a job is losing a connection to people, passion, and purpose. We will feel it.

Allow yourself to grieve for a while. Recognize that you will experience waves of emotions. Give yourself permission to treat a job loss like any other type of loss, because *it is* a loss. The process of grieving and acceptance is a very important and integral part of moving forward. **Grief comes in waves, but so does clarity.**

Facing and embracing grief allows us to experience the shock, anger, disappointment, and other feelings that need to be processed before we can move through this transition. We can allow things to settle down, trusting that we are exactly where we need to be at this time, in this space, going through this grieving process. Our purpose right now might be to stay in the discomfort and learn from it—we're learning patience and acceptance. Grieving is a time to talk about our feelings, not talk ourselves out of them.

Grief can stir up other emotions, many very intense, and it's okay to feel all of them. Feelings of guilt, fear, and sadness are a normal part of any grieving process. Take deep breaths and learn to be okay with sitting in the swamp for a while. Even while you are grieving, you can still be gentle and kind with yourself. Remain present and aware while you are grieving and be aware that you may be more sensitive or easily triggered as you work through your grief.

Grieving is not the time to evaluate your entire life. It's okay to leave other problems on the back burner to be solved at another time. This is your moment to be with your emotions.

The grieving phase is also an opportunity to seek wisdom from your resources: your go-to people, books, movies, music—whatever you use to reconnect with love, acceptance, friendship, wisdom, and support. Grieving is time for you to process what has happened, but you don't need to process alone.

> Jill was recently laid off and was having a difficult time. In her mind, the layoff was unnecessary and impersonal, and she didn't want to accept it.
>
> A week later, Jill received a note from a former

colleague (who was also laid off) inviting her to a get-together with their other laid-off peers. At first, Jill considered attending the event, but after giving it more thought, decided not to go. She just wanted to be alone right now. When she was ready to grieve with others, she would reach out.

Later that day, Jill had another burst of anger and frustration when she remembered that five of her customers were registered to attend one of her webinars in the coming week and she had no way of reaching them. Jill felt that her credibility was on the line, and this was disappointing and frustrating. What could she do? She had to let it go.

The following week, Jill met a close friend for coffee. Her friend listened attentively as Jill explained her frustrations. After they were done, Jill started to feel better; and by the end of the week, she began feeling even more relief. It felt like the fog was finally lifting.

That weekend, Jill thought about what her Mom had said to her the day she'd been laid off: "Just give it time." As she thought about her Mom's words, she took a series of deep breaths and focused on letting her anger go. Jill knew that with the help of her friends and family, and by giving herself more time to work through her grief, she would eventually get through this. She just needed to take it one step at a time.

REALITY CHECK

- Grieving is natural. Allow yourself to go through the process.
- Be kind and gentle with yourself as you grieve.
- Remember that this, too, shall pass.

QUESTIONS TO CONSIDER

1) As I've been grieving, which feelings have seemed natural? Which have surprised me?

2) How can I best support myself as I experience the grieving process?

INNER AFFIRMATIONS

"I am allowed to grieve about anything that has changed in my life, including this event. I realize that by processing the feelings associated with change, I can move into a healthy place within me where new creative energy will start to form."

Chapter 6 — Losing Your Anchors

Sometimes when you come to the end of yourself,
give yourself a chance to dig in deeper. Look for the good
and you'll find strength you never knew you had.
— Michelle Muriel

Have you ever had a temporary injury? For example, sprained your ankle, broken your arm, cut your hand, or suffered some other condition that forced you to change your daily routine? Suddenly, your *normal routine* stops and everything changes. It can be quite an adjustment.

The way we react to changes in our regular routines is important. Whether we realize it or not, the choices we make and subsequent results of those choices provide us with consistency, stability, and balance, a stable place that contributes to a sense of well-being. These qualities are different for each of us, but we all have them.

Just like the anchors on a boat, our personal anchors ground us and keep us stabilized. Things like job, health, and home become our physical anchors. We also have emotional anchors coming from the people in our lives who love and encourage us. Our anchors change over time as our perspectives change. Most of these anchor-moving life changes happen slowly and with our consent—most, but not all.

Unexpected change can be very difficult. When something as simple as having a consistent work schedule suddenly disappears, the rest of our lives can quickly go into disarray. A daily schedule gives us a sense of consistency and reliability, and when that is removed, it can be quite a shock.

A sudden layoff can also spark unexpected changes in our emotional anchors, leading to a loss of belonging. We might miss the daily social interactions with coworkers and the feeling of having a "work family." It can also strike at our sense of purpose: We might worry about the fate of a project, especially if the product or service it creates will help people in urgent need, or we might lose a sense of accomplishment from working in an industry that serves others. **Without anchors, we may feel lost.**

Wherever you are on the journey, you always have the ability to make positive and healthy choices. If you keep that in mind, then you can be more flexible when those anchors are uprooted. Change is difficult, but it can be managed when you stay aware of the power of your choices, even if it's simply your attitude.

> When Tammy was working full time, she had a regular weekly schedule that provided consistency and stability in her life. After Tammy was laid off, losing this anchor caused significant changes to her daily routine—in fact, there were times when she wasn't even sure what day it was. She felt like she had been set adrift, like a ship floating out on the open sea with no direction.
>
> With this loss of a daily schedule, Tammy found herself stuck in denial. She'd heard a suggestion from a friend about "taking a vacation from reality," so for the first

two weeks following her layoff, Tammy decided to take time off. She spent many of her days shopping at the mall, going out for dinner, and watching movies until the wee hours of the morning. Although at first it felt good to detach herself from her anger and disappointment, Tammy eventually started to feel guilty about ignoring the truth that she was still sad and disappointed.

Tammy realized she had a choice of how to respond to the layoff. She could continue to wallow in disappointment and self-pity, or she could use this opportunity to imagine a new path and chart a different course. But she also knew that creating new anchors takes time. As her friend Kathy told her, "Everyone begins at a different place. Start by recognizing where you are, and then decide where you want to go."

With some help from another friend who'd also been recently laid off, Tammy decided it was time to start making her job transition a priority. Creating new daily and weekly schedules would help her to establish a new point of focus—a new anchor, of sorts. Within the first few days of creating a new routine, Tammy started to feel better.

REALITY CHECK

- Creating new anchors is a continuous part of life.
- Change stirs up a lot of uncomfortable emotions for everyone, and you're not weak for feeling them.
- We have the power to choose our responses to what life hands us.

QUESTIONS TO CONSIDER

1) What and who are my current anchors?

2) How can a heightened awareness of my changing anchors help me during this transition?

INNER AFFIRMATIONS

"Losing my anchors can be difficult. But I have the inner courage and resources to overcome these challenges and create a new direction. I know that I am in a very powerful creative place right now and that I have nothing to fear; rather, I am excited about what I can and will create next."

CHAPTER 7 — GO WITH THE FLOW

> *Ancora Imparo: I am still learning.*
> — Michelangelo

Part of the transition process for any life change is learning how to be flexible and optimistic during difficult times. Change is constant. Things are always moving and expanding whether we see it or not, and sometimes it feels like change is happening **to** us, when in reality, change is happening **with** us. If we have courage to move with the change, we can *go with the flow* and become part of it rather than resisting.

To go with the flow is to allow the natural rhythm of life to work with us. A constant stream of well-being is always flowing to us and through us. Going with the flow lets us release resistance, relax, and float with the current. The concept of *allowing* teaches us to accept all things, including people, as they are right now—knowing that all things change with time.

Going with the flow requires patience and understanding. Through letting go, we can be both present and curious about the unknown while **trusting that everything we need to know and learn will be put in our path**. When things don't come quickly or easily to us, we can choose to honor the timing of things and add wishes to a *waiting patiently list*. With the power of positive thinking, doubt can shift into anticipation. Saying, "I don't know what's going to happen next... and that excites me," opens us up to welcoming the unexpected.

Especially when we are so focused on something as important as securing a new job, going with the flow allows us to exhale into the moment and release the need to control it. When we learn to accept the present moment and allow situations to be as they are, we experience the freedom to stay focused on ourselves. This is a critical skill to master during times of change.

> Doug was laid off from a company where he'd been working for over ten years. Although the news was a shock to him, his first thought was how he was going to tell his fiancé. Doug and Amy had been saving their money for the past two years so they could get married. But now he wasn't sure of anything. He felt like the whole world had stopped. He couldn't imagine what he was going to do now.
>
> That evening, Doug and Amy sat down to discuss the situation. While Amy listened, Doug expressed his anger and disappointment about losing his job and his fear about what was going to happen next. Amy shared a different perspective with him. "Do you realize this is an opportunity for something new?" she said. "You've been saying for years that you didn't really like that job anyway, so now you can take some time to explore more about what you really want to do. Let's not worry about it. Let's just go with the flow."
>
> Even though Doug was still frustrated, he knew deep inside that Amy was right. Perhaps this was the right time for new career direction.

The next day, Doug sat down at the kitchen table with pen and paper and started writing some ideas about his new career path. He decided to slow down the job-hunting process; focus on getting himself organized; take things step-by-step; and not worry about what would happen next. Doug realized this change was a very timely and positive opportunity for him to create a new direction for himself. Through this experience, he learned the power of *going with the flow*: that change is something to appreciate, not fear.

REALITY CHECK

- Going with the flow can allow us to slow down the process of transition and take a more deliberate approach.
- Learning to go with the flow facilitates trust in the process and in ourselves.
- Our challenge is to be content in the present moment and allow the flow to take us wherever we need to go.

QUESTIONS TO CONSIDER

1) In what ways am I following the flow of events?

2) In what ways am I resisting them?

INNER AFFIRMATIONS

"I am able to choose my thoughts and actions with wise and conscious intention. I realize that change is a constant part of life, and so I choose to move with it instead of pushing against it. I am flexible and I can go with the flow easily and effortlessly."

PART II:
ALIGNMENT

Get to Know Yourself

CHAPTER 8 — WORK SMARTER, NOT HARDER

In a way, I have simplified my life by setting priorities.
— Karen Duffy

Immediately following a layoff or the decision to transition your career, you may experience a sense of urgency to run out and find another job as quickly as possible. Although these feelings are natural—coming from our fear-based brain—an alternative is to give yourself more time to process. There is tremendous benefit to taking the time to re-invest in yourself and reprioritize your activities as you recreate your career direction.

When it comes to searching for a new career, what do you consider *hard work*? If your main goal is to find a new job as quickly as possible, you might miss out on important aspects of the process that could help your job search be more productive.

You might define *hard work* as spending six to eight hours on your computer job searching each day; trying to fit in as many lunches and coffees as you can; or skimping on meals, family time, or exercise. This response will certainly create action, but will these actions create the results that you really want? While the concept of "working harder" can bring results, it can also distract us from remembering our priorities, recognizing unproductive effort, or engaging in balanced behaviors. **Working harder keeps us busy; working smarter keeps us productive**.

We can produce powerful results without exerting as much effort by thinking carefully through priorities, deliberately planning activities, and aligning ourselves with specific goals before taking action. Working smarter means knowing our limitations, developing healthy and effective boundaries, and learning to love and respect ourselves enough to grow from our experience.

Part of sifting through the variety of choices available to us requires that we use our power of discernment. Discernment includes activating intuition and our deepest instincts when making decisions. When we are sensitive to the longer-term effects of our actions, discernment allows us to make a potentially different choice. Often, our first response may not be the best one. Discernment reminds us that sometimes it is beneficial to step back and *soften our stance*—to reconsider our approach—before we choose, keeping in mind that we can always choose again.

While searching for new employment, continue to gather data, ask questions, and regroup with yourself. Check in with your thoughts, feelings, and intuition on a regular basis and take that information into consideration as well.

- What are your thoughts about your job search and the next opportunity?
- What are your feelings?
- What do your gut instincts tell you?

If you are unsure, wait until you have more information or feel a nudge in one direction or another before you act. For example, instead of applying for jobs you don't really want, wait until you feel an inner alignment with an opportunity. This can save hours of unproductive and wasted effort. In addition, you will honor yourself and your intentions by being selective.

Since her layoff six months ago, Amy had decided to focus on picking up occasional contract work while starting to build her own business. She'd been to a couple of career classes and as suggested by a former colleague, started writing down her priorities. Identifying these preferences would help Amy affirm and re-establish her preferences and give her a way of communicating that to recruiters.

One day, Amy received a call from a contract company telling her about a new opportunity. As the recruiter explained details of the contract, Amy started to compare them to her desired preferences. At first, the contract sounded good: designing new training for teachers, nearby location, and a decent hourly rate. At first, Amy felt good about the potential opportunity.

Then Amy asked if the contract was short duration (less than six months) and if the client allowed for flexible hours—two important preferences that Amy had flagged as potential "deal breakers" as she was building her new business. The recruiter told her that this was a long-term contract and the client wanted the contractor on-site working a standard 8-5, Monday-Friday schedule.

This did not excite Amy. She told the recruiter she'd need to think about it. Her gut feeling was telling her to wait.

Three days later, another contract company called Amy about an opportunity that was a much better fit:

flexible hours, short-term contract, and Amy could create her own schedule. In addition, the pay was higher! Amy was glad that she had listened to her intuition and waited before accepting the first opportunity.

REALITY CHECK

- Working smarter requires attention and focus.
- Discernment is a powerful prioritization tool.
- If you are unsure about something, wait until you know how to respond.

QUESTIONS TO CONSIDER

1) In what areas of my life am I working smarter?

2) What is an area where I need to soften my stance?

INNER AFFIRMATIONS

"I am aware of my energy and I am able to discern when I am trying too hard to make something happen. I know that I can always take a step back, soften my stance, and re-think my approach to anything or to anyone. I am able to follow the natural flow of my creative energy and work more intelligently."

CHAPTER 9 — WHO ARE YOU?

When a great ship is in harbor and moored, it is safe, there can be no doubt. But that is not what great ships are built for.
— Clarissa Pinkola Estes, Ph.D.

The words, *"Know thyself"* were inscribed on the entrance to the Temple of Apollo at Delphi thousands of years ago. Recognizing your potential and learning from your life experience are as valuable for us as they were for the ancient Greeks. Knowing yourself means knowing your strengths and limitations; that you have powerful thoughts, feelings, and intuition; and that you are continually creating your own life experience.

When you know yourself, you can live in truth and transparency in all areas of your life, even during challenging times. Since a career transition is a time that's filled with so many unknowns, the more you know about your emotional well-being, the better. When you have taken the time to think about *who you are and what you do well*, the easier it will be to know what type of a career opportunity you'd like to create next.

Knowing yourself can contribute to a sense of purpose— the feeling that you are here for a reason and have a role to fulfill. Purpose gives our lives meaning and contributes to an overall sense of worthiness. Feeling an internal sense of purpose can give us direction and help with decision-making, especially when choosing our career path.

**Knowing yourself means being aware
of your potential and trusting that
you are always growing into it.**

After a layoff, it is natural to feel self-doubt and confusion for a period of time. But as you get some distance from your former job, you may discover that you have a fresh view of who you are and what you love to do. Looking back over your work, ask yourself what your strengths are and what you'd like to improve.

Begin by reviewing your current resume or work history:

- What have you done? What experiences have you had?
- What do you enjoy doing?
- What are you good at?
- What do you wish you could be doing at work?

Answering these questions will assist you in getting to know yourself even better, especially the person who you are *right now*.

Another way to learn more about yourself is to solicit input from others. Other people see us differently than we see ourselves because it is impossible for us to see ourselves objectively. Asking people with whom you've worked to give you feedback about your top traits can be a very good way to identify your areas of strength and expertise. This action demonstrates trust and respect for their opinion. Reaching out to others and allowing them to help you in a time of need is also a gesture of gratitude.

As I was going through a job transition a few years ago, I interviewed for a contract training position with a relatively young technology company. Even though I wasn't interested in contract work at the time, many things about the position intrigued me, so I applied and got an interview.

During my interview, I met with the CEO and the Vice President. After we had confirmed that my experience and expertise were directly aligned with the skills and talents they sought, I asked them what support they currently had in place for training. They showed me some of their sales brochures and product guides. I told them, "That's not training."

Since I had taken the time to learn about my natural skills and abilities, I knew that I felt comfortable facilitating a challenging discussion. I also knew that I could visually represent my ideas in a effective way, so I drew out the job description on a whiteboard. I then proceeded to explain how they needed to build a training platform and infrastructure, including materials and processes. I was showing my training expertise and telling them what they didn't know. They were surprised and impressed.

After some negotiation with the company and the recruiter, I was able to turn the contract position into a full-time job and start the job within two weeks. By knowing myself—that I am an educator and an expert in my field—I was able to articulate that knowledge to meet their needs and create a job that supported who I am and what I love to do.

REALITY CHECK

- The better we know ourselves, the more we can identify and communicate our talents and strengths.
- A good way to learn more about ourselves is to ask for feedback from others.
- Job transition is another opportunity to create what we want to do and who we want to be.

QUESTIONS TO CONSIDER

1) Who am I and what do I do well?

2) How are my belief systems helping or hurting me?

INNER AFFIRMATIONS

"I realize that I have the potential to look at my past experiences and really get to know myself and my purpose. With this expanded knowledge, I can demonstrate my skills with confidence and ease."

CHAPTER 10 — DREAMING OUT LOUD

When your gifts and passion align,
therein lies your purpose.
— Renee Rongen

When we were small children, we were often taught to dream big, a common form of possibility thinking. It is a way of encouraging kids to not limit themselves and their potential. So why do we stop reinforcing that with adults? Is there an assumption that adults have it "all figured out" and no longer need to keep dreaming?

The truth is that we are always reinventing ourselves and, therefore, we should never stop dreaming. You would think that we should be getting smarter and more creative as we age, as we are constantly learning new things. As adults we may be taught that dreaming is silly and pointless, when in reality, dreaming is an essential part of creating a new experience—and this is especially important during a job transition. The ability to reconnect to our dreams is always available to us.

Part of the alignment process during job transition is to actively articulate what we desire and *dream out loud*. If you look at the definition of a dream according to

Merriam-Webster, it is "something that you have wanted very much to do, be, or have for a long time." What better opportunity to re-examine your dreams than during a major life transition?

Dreaming out loud can harness the power of passion. Discovering passion starts with awareness:

- What motivates you?
- What makes you feel really great while you're doing it?
- What have you always wanted to do, but haven't had the chance?

Passion is always inside of us—we just need to pay attention and notice what it feels like.

Do you think passion has a role in the workplace? According to research, passionate people are twice as likely to be energized or inspired by unexpected challenges in the workplace than those who are disengaged. This is a prime indicator that being passionate about what we do and who we are makes a difference. It has also been found that passionate employees seek to stimulate new thinking and creativity—and what company doesn't need more creativity?!

We can connect with our passion more easily when we are in alignment with our gifts and talents. Passion is a part of *who we already are*. Reconnecting with our happiness will help bring more passion into our lives.

> **If our interests are aligned with our passions,
> then our gifts and talents shine even brighter.**

Kathleen always wanted to be a gourmet chef. When she was 12 years old, she saw Julia Child on television cooking an elaborate feast for a group of French dignitaries. Kathleen was hooked. During her high school and college years, Kathleen focused on academics, graduated from college with a degree in finance, and took a job as an accountant. Kathleen became very successful in her accounting career, but food was still her passion.

Unfortunately, Kathleen was laid off from her accounting position. She took advantage of the money available for education through her unemployment benefits package and enrolled in cooking school. During the first class, each student introduced themselves and their reason for joining the program. Kathleen shared her dream out loud with the group and for the first time in her life, felt that her dream could, indeed, come true. After an eighteen-month program, Kathleen graduated with her degree in Culinary Arts.

During lunch with friends shortly afterward, a former co-worker mentioned that a friend was forming a part-time catering business and looking for someone to help with the cooking. She suggested that Kathleen contact her. Within a week, Kathleen found herself cooking an elaborate feast for a group of local businesswomen at a weekend retreat. The event was so successful that Kathleen was asked to become the primary chef for all of their future events. Her dream had come true.

REALITY CHECK

- People of any age can dream out loud.
- Passion comes from within and can be activated by dreaming out loud.
- Connecting with our passion is easier when we are in alignment with ourselves.

QUESTIONS TO CONSIDER

1) In what ways can dreaming out loud create momentum for new opportunities?

2) How can I include what I am passionate about in my work?

INNER AFFIRMATIONS

"I am aware of my dreams and deliberately set my direction by dreaming out loud about what I want to create in my life. I know that my dreams come from deep within me, so I will take the time to listen within, tap my passions, and follow my quiet inner voice. With this knowledge, I can confidently activate my desires and dreams out loud."

CHAPTER 11 — FINDING CLARITY

Life is not about finding yourself.
Life is about creating yourself.
— George Bernard Shaw

The next step toward coming into alignment with who you are is to clarify your intentions and preferences. The objective here is to reflect on your past experiences and what you've learned and then apply those lessons to help move you forward. Having golden nuggets of your *own* wisdom from success stories as well as lessons learned helps you to communicate who you are and the value you bring to an organization.

Intentions are the direct reflection of your deepest truth and belief systems; they form the foundation for your attitudes, actions, and words. Intentions move values from thought into word, word into action, and action into being.

Finding the true heart of your intentions starts by asking yourself what you *really* want. Sometimes this is clearest when you are experiencing what you *don't want*. Contrasting your experiences will help you to create what you *do want*. In fact, **some of your most powerful intentions are born in your moments of greatest contrast.**

Intentions are more than just wishful thinking. Before intentions can shift into reality, we have to express them. The act of speaking intentions aloud shifts them from dreaming to doing. Whenever we express our thoughts and feelings, something always happens.

Another way to gain clarity while focusing your attention is to establish priorities, including what you want and don't want with regard to the environments, people, type of leadership, and nature of the work you are seeking. By using your past experience as your guide, you can quickly and easily determine priorities moving forward.

Knowing your preferences and backing them up with poignant examples and stories will show an employer that you truly know yourself. This will also facilitate the alignment process and make it easier for both you and the employer to see if you are a good fit for the position. See *Appendix B: Personal Priority Grid (PPG)*.

> Six weeks after Lauren's layoff from her job with a Fortune 25 company, the fog of confusion and disappointment was finally starting to clear. After getting through a challenging grieving process, she was grateful for the friends and family who had stood beside her as she processed her disappointment.
>
> While reading a private Facebook page created for people who had been laid off, Lauren saw a posting for *The White Box Club*—a support group created to provide tools and resources to people in career transition. She felt the nudge to check it out, so she attended her first meeting the next week.
>
> The day Lauren attended, we were discussing a useful tool called a Personal Priority Grid, or PPG—a simple spreadsheet meant to help people clarify their personal priorities. By identifying what you *do want*, *don't want*,

and what you're *willing to accept* in a new job, you can quickly hone-in on intentions, establish priorities, and create the foundation for developing the language to speak about your preferences. Lauren liked the idea.

That evening, she started to fill out her PPG and identify what she really wanted. This simple exercise gave her some much-needed clarity and helped her to quickly identify her intentions and priorities. The PPG became the primary tool Lauren used to update her resume and it helped to prompt relevant stories and examples that she could use during the interviewing process.

By keeping her PPG updated, Lauren had a template to continue getting *even clearer* about what she wanted to create in her new job. She realized the great value that this tool could bring to her career search—and life— moving forward.

REALITY CHECK

- You have the ability to focus and improve your clarity about who you are and what you really want.
- Knowing what you want will help you establish priorities.
- The clearer you are about what you want, the easier it will be to create the language to tell others about it.

QUESTIONS TO CONSIDER

1) In which areas of my life do I have clarity?

2) Which areas are not so clear?

INNER AFFIRMATIONS

"All of my experiences, including this challenge, are teaching me more about myself and what is important to me. I am getting clearer every day about what I want and what I don't want, so I can use that information to make better decisions and communicate them more clearly to others."

CHAPTER 12 — SETTING A DIRECTION

One's destination is never a place,
but rather a new way of looking at things.
— Henry Miller

Exploring our passions and intentions will help us cultivate the feelings that can jumpstart career transition. Taking inventory of our strengths and creating a vision ignites the fuel to propel our dreams and intentions into reality.

Strengths refer to our knowledge, skills, and abilities. Strengths can be identified by paying attention to where our gifts and talents are used most effectively or when we have education and training in a particular area of expertise. In addition, useful evaluation and assessment tools can help us identify our areas of strength and, with this knowledge, direct ourselves towards opportunities that support them.

When we combine the knowledge of our strengths with our passions and intentions, we can start to create a vision. A vision is a clear statement of purpose that refines our focus; for example, "My vision is to provide speaking and coaching support to all of my customers so they can make healthy, balanced, and informed decisions."

Having a vision brings clarity to our purpose and helps create a foundation upon which all of our other goals and objectives are based. A vision grounds us. A personal vision can be just as powerful as a company vision. If we are aligned with our strengths, intentions, and passion, our vision will come.

Since the mind cannot discriminate between dreaming and reality, a personal vision can create very powerful results. Creating a vision will help us to align with our feelings. Feelings are feedback and indicators of what is, or is not, in alignment with our intentions. Following our feelings will always lead us to the thoughts and actions that are in alignment with our deepest truths, and our vision will be the outcome.

Envision in your mind's eye what brings you joy. What are you doing? Where are you? Who is there? How are you feeling? This will help to create a vision. Now, translate that feeling into a work environment. What type of activities will elicit those feelings? What are you doing? Where are you doing it, and with whom? Once you have this vision, think about how you can bring that into a career choice.

> Ever since David joined a commercial design firm, his dream was to someday create and manage his own business. Over the years, David learned the ins and outs of the design business and built a solid portfolio. He started developing good habits for building relationships, managing accounts, and collaborating with his boss and design team to ensure that their clients were always satisfied.
>
> After five years with the firm, David was unexpectedly

laid off during a business restructuring initiative. Although the layoff was quite a shock, he knew deep down inside that this was his opportunity to move into his vision.

Part of David's unemployment benefits included a program entitled *Building Your Business Plan*, a state-funded re-employment program designed to help budding entrepreneurs start their own businesses. Part of that course was to create a vision. Since David had been dreaming of creating his own design firm for so many years, he knew exactly where to start. He took an inventory of his knowledge, skills, and abilities and studied how they could be applied to his new vision.

After completing the six-month program, David officially opened his own company. By applying what he had learned during the inventory process—along with his newly developed business acumen—he fell easily into alignment with the transition to his new business. Within the first year, David was making more money than he had working for his previous firm, and this time, he was running the show!

Reality Check

- Taking inventory of your knowledge, skills, and abilities helps you to define your strengths.
- Feelings are feedback about what is, or is not, in alignment with our intentions.
- What drives you can become part of your vision.

Questions to Consider

1) How does being aware of my strengths help me with my career path?

2) In what ways could creating a vision benefit me?

Inner Affirmations

"I have valuable knowledge, skills, and abilities, and I can apply them easily in whatever career direction I choose. I know that taking inventory of my skills and creating a vision will always benefit me, and the career I manifest will be a direct reflection of the strengths, talents, and creative passions that I have inside me."

The White Box Club Handbook | **59**

CHAPTER 13 — YOU'VE GOT BENEFITS

*Unless you do something beyond what you
have already mastered, you will never grow.*
— Ralph Waldo Emerson

Along with financial support services, a great number of benefit programs have been designed for people in career transition. These programs have been established in our cities, counties, and states, and like unemployment insurance, are funded by state and federal tax dollars. These benefits have been put in place to support individuals, spouses, children, and other extended family members when they need it most.

Career placement and re-employment benefits are the most common support services used by people who have been laid off or are in career transition. Each county and state has a wide variety of career readiness and placement programs designed to assist participants with their job search. Services range from support for career exploration; job-hunting, networking, resume and cover letter writing, and interviewing techniques; to specific one-on-one career counseling sessions.

Most benefit programs have funds allocated for free training and work skill development—either to help you strengthen your skills in your current job field, or to help you explore new career opportunities. Sector-based training programs give people the credentials to find new jobs in growing career fields such as manufacturing, healthcare, customer service, and transportation.

In addition, some programs offer educational subsidies paired with extensive employment counseling and support assistance (such as covering transportation costs with bus passes or gift cards for purchasing new work clothes). The ultimate goal of these programs is to not only prepare their participants, but also to place them into full-time employment—even if it's a new career path.

Along with employment support, benefit programs also provide personal support—giving people hope in times of emotional distress. Professional counselors are available to help individuals, spouses, children, and entire families to process their feelings and get through the transition process. As layoffs and job changes continue to become more frequent, we can expect to see more growth and expansion in these areas.

If you have been laid off, you may automatically receive re-employment and job search benefits as part of your severance package. If not, there are plenty of information resources available online through your city and state web sites. Be sure to check with your local re-employment office regarding the programs and services available to you in your location.

> Tim had been working in the travel industry for nearly ten years when he was laid off. Although he was shocked at first, he wasn't too surprised. His travel agency had taken a nosedive in the past few years, and there were other travel companies who were also

laying off workers. Tim figured he was lucky to have kept a job as long as he did.

After the layoff, Tim thought about his work history, and although he liked his work, he thought this might be a good time to try something new. As part of his severance package, he was encouraged to attend a re-employment session. There he learned about the support services available for people seeking new career directions, including training and education support. It was then that Tim knew the timing was right to make a change.

Since he'd always been interested in healthcare, Tim inquired about the certification program for a health navigator—a new type of customer service position. The county program coordinator told him more about the program, the 8-week training course, and the wide array of opportunities that would be available to him after certification. And as part of the re-employment program, Tim learned that he was eligible for 100% coverage of the program expenses.

Tim enrolled in the certification program and was ready to start the journey towards his new career. He was grateful for the opportunity to follow his new interest, and he knew that someday he might look back at his layoff as a blessing in disguise. This would never have occurred to him a few months ago.

REALITY CHECK

- There are an abundance of free tools and resources available to people in transition.
- Benefits may include anything from tuition assistance to bus passes and gift cards.
- There is support available for starting a career in a new industry or area of interest.

QUESTIONS TO CONSIDER

1) How am I using the benefits available to me? And if not, why not?

2) What could I gain from these benefits in relationship to my career development?

INNER AFFIRMATIONS

"There is an abundance of help and support available to me right now. There are many re-employment and educational benefits already in place, and I have only to learn how to optimize their use. I have plenty of resources to support my education and career development when I need them."

CHAPTER 14 — RESUME REFRESH

What you get by achieving your goals is not as important
as what you become by achieving your goals.
— Zig Ziglar

Once you have invested your effort into finding clarity, dreaming out loud, and taking personal inventory of your knowledge, skills, and abilities, you are ready to refresh your resume.

Many people think a resume is just a document of your previous employment and education history. But the resume is actually more like a business card—a professional introduction containing an overview of who you are and what you've done.

The goal of an effective resume is to create a clean, organized summary of your work history and make a potential employer want to learn more about you and how you might fit within their organization. A good resume does not need to contain a huge amount of detail, but it does need to explain potentially complex information in a simple and easy-to-follow format.

Keep in mind that the resume is a document, not an interview. Once you've transcribed who you are, what you've done, and what you'd like to do next, you still need to be able to speak about yourself and walk a recruiter or interviewer through your resume. That is why it is so important to take the time to create a clean, sharp, and succinct resume.

There are many different styles and types of resumes, the most common including:

- **Chronological:** suggested for job seekers with little work history
- **Functional:** suggested for job seekers with specific accomplishments in various areas
- **Hybrid/integrated**: suggested for job seekers with a history of a varied jobs in several different areas or career paths

There is also an abundance of resources available to help you write, edit, and refine your resume. In fact, many re-employment programs include free support for resume writing and editing, so be sure to check out what is available to you.

Some elements of a good resume include:

- A statement of *who you are and what you want to do* (for example, "Technology Educator with over 15 years of experience seeking a full-time position in Technology Education and Leadership development with a Fortune 50 corporation")
- Your top three areas of expertise (for example, Project Management, Technology Education, and Strategic Planning Development)
- Three or four bullets below each topic area highlighting accomplishments from your previous job experiences

- Measureable accomplishments, using numbers, percentages, and statistics whenever possible (for example, "Exceeded projected goals by increasing program participation by over 400% in 12 months")
- A list of your previous employment, education, and any relevant awards or accomplishment within the past 15 years (experiences older than 15 years can be listed as "other employment" and without dates)

For more detailed tips about writing your resume, see *Appendix C: Resume Tip Sheet.*

In addition, your resume is a roadmap of your career path. The resume and PPG are useful tools when you are defining what you would like to do next in your career. They create a platform on which you can build your career and continue to refine your preferences as you map your direction.

Heidi hadn't updated her resume in over 20 years. Why should she? She was secure in her job, and when she was originally hired she was told she had a "job for life." But when the company was acquired two decades later, Heidi faced a layoff.

After getting over her initial shock and disappointment, Heidi started to put herself back together. As part of her unemployment benefits, she took a resume writing class. During the course, Heidi learned how to refresh her resume by adding relevant examples and accomplishments; her old resume had simply listed job responsibilities. She also learned about resume scanning software and how it searches on keywords; Heidi researched the best keywords for her profession and added them into her resume where appropriate.

The course also taught her how her resume could

become a great communication tool. By organizing and updating her resume on a regular basis, she could keep a fresh perspective on her past accomplishments while staying focused on her ideas for the future.

Heidi had learned firsthand how the act of updating her resume helped her to know more about herself, gain clarity on her strengths and accomplishments, and feel a sense of pride about her past work history. She now understood how a resume was more than just a summary; it was a tool to help guide her to the next career opportunity.

REALITY CHECK

- Your resume is a business card.
- Find your language; use your keywords.
- When it comes to resumes: Less is more; simple is better.

QUESTIONS TO CONSIDER

1) Who am I and what skills, strengths, and accomplishments do I offer employers?

2) What sets me apart from others? What makes me unique?

INNER AFFIRMATIONS

"My resume is a direct reflection of who I am and what I bring to the world. I know that with work and focus, I will be able to create a resume that is clear and concise and features me in a positive and appealing light. My resume will be the best written representation of me and my career that there is."

PART III:
ACTIVATION

Make It Happen!

CHAPTER 15 — REDRAWING YOUR MAP

You are never too old to set another
goal or to dream a new dream.
— C. S. Lewis

Each point in our lives begins a new opportunity to choose again, especially during times of great change. When life catches us by surprise, we are challenged to make decisions based on very little information. This puts us quickly into a learning mode. As we continue to activate our choices and exercise our critical thinking skills, we can start to naturally come into alignment with our true selves.

You are now ready to start *redrawing your map.* So what does that mean?

Redrawing your map means exploring your options from the perspective of your passions, intentions, and purpose rather than allowing outside factors or assumptions to limit your choices. You begin the creative process within you, choosing to create your world from the *inside out.* When you start to make choices by activating your intuition first, not last, you align your intentions in this search with your spiritual energy—the source of your creativity.

Logistically, you are preparing to enter into activation mode in your career transition. You have already identified what you want and don't want in a new career. As you are thinking about your new direction, recall the aspects of former jobs that you liked or appreciated— perhaps it was your coworkers, customers, or the environment in which you were working. Add these to your PPG so you have them written down and clarified. This will give you solid examples to draw from as you create a new map and set a destination.

Another critical aspect of redrawing your map is to continue following your intuitive "nudges"—those gut feelings of being *called towards something or intrigued by it.* Recognizing and following these subtle signals can keep broadening your options in a career search and give you permission to explore new and potentially different possibilities.

Sometimes curiosity can lead us to things we've been dreaming about. It can be the pathway to those dreams that might not be familiar. Redrawing our maps gives us the creative freedom to create something new.

> Beth was laid off from her full-time job. Even though the layoff was disappointing, it wasn't a surprise. Her store had been making cutbacks every year, and when it was time for her department to make adjustments, Beth was included in the cuts. But after working in retail for over ten years, she was ready for change.

> When Beth sat down and started to redraw her map, she thought about how working in retail had helped her strengthen many of her skills, especially working with customers. In fact, she realized that working with her customers was the best part of her previous job. She thought about how she could take that positive experience into her next career opportunity.

While attending a job fair, Beth stopped by a booth representing the Department of Motor Vehicles (DMV). Like many others, Beth dreaded visits to the DMV with its long lines, excessive waiting, and busy counter staff. However, the hiring manager at the booth, Sharon, appeared friendly and polite. Beth thought to herself, *Now why isn't **this** woman working behind the counter at **my** DMV?*

Then Beth felt a nudge. Perhaps her love of working with customers was exactly what they needed at any DMV. Wouldn't she want her own experience to be a positive one? Beth asked Sharon for more information and ended up applying for a job online that evening. Within one week, Beth was asked to come and interview, and two weeks later was offered a job in customer service.

Within the first month of employment, Beth received three compliments that went straight to Sharon, praising Beth as the kindest DMV clerk they had ever experienced. Sharon was supportive and recognized Beth at the next monthly staff meeting. Beth felt appreciated for *what she did* and *who she is*. She also realized that her cheerful personality had helped her find purpose in a new work environment.

Being willing to explore new options gave Beth a new opportunity to feel good about herself and her work.

REALITY CHECK

- The creative process begins within you.
- You always have the ability to recreate your direction.
- Redrawing your map can mean exploring new and different possibilities.

QUESTIONS TO CONSIDER

1) Which direction feels good to me right now? What feels right?

2) When have I experienced a nudge and where did that lead me?

INNER AFFIRMATIONS

"I can create whichever direction I choose, and I can course-correct or change direction at any time along my journey. I recognize and acknowledge that I have an internal guidance system—my intuition—and it can assist me with finding new and creative ways of fulfilling my purpose in my work and life."

Chapter 16 — The Power of Choice

> *Your life does not get better by chance.*
> *It gets better by change.*
> — Jim Rohn

One of our biggest gifts is the ability to choose. In every moment we choose where to focus our attention and energy—and most importantly, how to respond to what is happening around us. The outcomes of our choices, in turn, create our realities.

Our lives are filled with a constant stream of choices, and our choices are always changing. Technology has given us access to real-time information—which means we can now be constantly bombarded with an onslaught of new choices. With this explosion of information has come the problem of *choice overload*.

Luckily, our power to choose includes our ability to unplug when necessary; to walk away from our computer; to put down our mobile phone; to turn off the TV; to say, "No thank you, I need some quiet time." It's always our choice.

Particularly during challenging times—such as during career transition—the outcomes of your choices will be extremely important. When you are in a position of great change, you might feel pressured to make hasty decisions and not take the time to think about the impacts of those choices. However, with a little thought and deliberate intent, you can slow down your thoughts, connect with your feelings, and make balanced choices in alignment with your intentions.

We can deliberately choose our actions, of course, but choosing our *reactions* are just as important. Newton's Law reminds us that "to every action there is a reaction." We are all naturally wired to be reactive—a function of the human brain designed to protect the body from harm. But it is our ability to *respond* to our reactions that activates our power of choice. For example, when someone is angry and yells at us, our natural reaction might be to yell back. However, taking a moment to stop and realize that we can choose our response can allow us to respond by stating our perspective without yelling or being forceful—actions that will not "fuel the fire." **Reacting is natural; responding is thoughtful.**

Like actions, our words can also have immediate results. Take, for instance, the words *No* and *Yes*. They're merely words—yet they provide powerful direction and feedback regarding our choices.

Attitude is also a choice. Is the glass half empty or half full? Is this transition a crisis or a catharsis? For many, a layoff or career transition may eventually become a blessing in disguise. There is a tremendous power in our perspective.

The power to create your experience is always in your hands. There will be times when you are directly in alignment with your vision and there will be times when you are unsure. If you are paying attention, the outcomes of your choices will give you powerful feedback regarding your alignment.

Whether you make good decisions or not, you need to respect and support yourself—believing that you are making the best choices with the information that you have at the moment. If later down the line you realize you didn't make the best choice and the outcome of your decision did not turn out favorably, you have the opportunity to accept the outcome as a learning experience. You can live in the knowledge that next time you are faced with a similar decision, you can make a different choice. You can always choose again.

> Kiernon had been working for a large Fortune 500 corporation for many years; he enjoyed his job and his coworkers and made a decent wage. But deep inside, he knew that he wanted more out of his career. He had done some creative writing and short film production in the past, but couldn't imagine how that could be created into a full-time career—not from where he was professionally positioned at the moment.
>
> Then Kiernon was laid off. During his transition period, he met with many people including Mark, a career coach. Kiernon told Mark his dream about being successful enough to leave the corporate world and making writing his primary career. Mark reminded him that he had some important choices: namely, to think "and" instead of "or." If Kiernon wanted to strengthen his writing career, he could start working towards that now, during his transition, AND still search for corporate work. This was a choice that Kiernon hadn't thought of before.
>
> Two months later, Kiernon was interviewing for a new

job in the corporate world. Taking into account his PPG, he considered the scope of the new job responsibilities knowing that he would also be writing outside of work. This helped Kiernon feel more comfortable about taking responsibility to meet his current obligations while he built the foundation for his writing dream.

REALITY CHECK

- The power to choose is our greatest gift.
- Not choosing is a choice. In the words of Neal Pert of Rush, "If you choose not to decide, you still have made a choice."
- We can always choose again.

QUESTIONS TO CONSIDER

1) What am I paying attention to that's working well for me right now? Not so well?

2) How can I activate my power to make better choices about my career transition?

INNER AFFIRMATIONS

"I know that I have the ability to choose and that my experiences directly correlate with my choices. I realize that I am the creator of my own reality, and that anytime I make a choice that results in an outcome that doesn't please me, I can always choose again."

CHAPTER 17 — GROWING YOUR NETWORK

Invisible threads are the strongest ties.
— Friedrich Nietzsche

Human beings are naturally wired for connection and affection. We're not here to live our lives alone, and we thrive best in collaboration with others. Connecting with new people inspires new ideas and new perspectives and freshens our outlook.

The most important aspect of creating an effective network is to get out and meet people. Even though you can make initial connections online, deeper relationships normally will not develop fully without a face-to-face connection. In addition, meeting with people in person helps you practice building a natural rapport with others. A meet-and-greet for lunch or coffee with a colleague can create an opportunity for you to practice your "elevator speech" and prepare for the interviewing process. Plus, you can ask your colleague for feedback and suggestions to improve your approach.

Networking for personal benefits has many perks. It helps to build new connections through which you can share information, answer questions, and find support.

Professionally, however, networking isn't only helpful, it is *mandatory*. Business networking supports collaboration with internal teams or making connections outside of the organization. Once you have established a business connection, you have set the foundation for sharing a multitude of resources ranging from best practices to collaborating on joint ventures and projects.

**Your business networks can be
your most valuable resources.**

Now that you have more clarity on what you want to be doing, you are ready to start networking. A helpful approach is to think about the people you know and whom *they* know. Learn the names of people who have the type of job you want, and then ask your network to help you meet those people for lunch or coffee. It has been stated that today, 70% to 80% of all new jobs are found by word of mouth. Your connections are your entry point to this inside network of opportunities.

When you meet with someone new, ask him or her about their experience. People are usually happy to tell their story, and sometimes the road they have taken is quite different from what you'd expect! Listen attentively and ask questions. Then tell them what you are looking for and ask their advice on getting there.

In closing, give them your business card and offer to send them your resume; ask for recommendations about whom you could talk to next. They might even make the introduction for you. After the meeting, don't forget to send a thank-you note or email!

The most important aspect of networking is the relationships that you form with others. Trust and alignment should be *primary*; what you can do for each other should be *secondary*. A truly healthy network is always based on balanced relationships founded on trust and respect for each other and the sharing of mutual gifts.

Refresh your network on a regular basis and don't wait until you *need* them before you invest time and energy in the people who support you. Asking to meet with people and catching up on a semi-regular basis can do this proactively. In addition, let people know that you are available to help them and *pay it forward*. When we share of our time and talents, everyone wins!

> Early in my professional career, I established a core network of fellow colleagues who knew me well and developed trust in me. When people needed my help, I always made myself available to them in the best way I could, and so many of them have reached out to me in return. My trusted network has always been there for me—especially during my numerous career transitions.
>
> Before I was laid off, I offered one free hour of career coaching to people in my trusted network who were in career transition. I wanted an opportunity to give back support to those who'd supported me.
>
> After I was laid off, I announced my own need for support at a networking meeting, and the response I received from my network colleagues was incredible. By the end of the meeting, I had received several leads on contracting or consulting opportunities. This response was an affirmation of the benefits of having a healthy and supportive network and made me feel grateful.

REALITY CHECK

- 70% to 80% of all new jobs are found by word of mouth.

- Networking will become easier the more you do it.

- Keep your network fresh at all times. Don't wait until you "need" them!

QUESTIONS TO CONSIDER

1) How is my networking helping with my career needs?

2) In what ways can I keep my network fresh?

INNER AFFIRMATIONS

"I understand the power of making connections with others, and I have the ability to create and maintain a healthy and productive network. I have done the work and become very clear about who I am and what I bring to the table, and I can speak to anyone about it clearly and without hesitation."

See *Appendix D: Networking Tip Sheet*

CHAPTER 18 — INTERVIEWING TO SHINE

> *The meaning of life is to find your gift.*
> *The purpose of life is to give it away.*
> — Pablo Picasso

If you think of the resume as a business card, then the interview is the face-to-face report—the opportunity to provide details, examples, and stories to supplement your career highlights. The interview is the most important aspect of the hiring process. If you have advanced to the interview stage, it's a good sign that the employer wants to hire you—they want to compare you to the other candidates and keep an eye out for any red flags.

An updated resume will help you speak to your past experiences quickly and easily. However, preparing to speak about you is only part of the equation. As you prepare for the interview, it is important that you study the company as well. Part of your research may include answering the following questions:

- What is their business?
- What is their mission? Vision?
- What do you like about the organization?
- And, ultimately, *why* do you want to work for them?

The real goal in the interview is to get to know more about one another and look for the best alignment for both parties. Consider that *you are interviewing them just as much as they are interviewing you.* From your perspective, think about alignment: Is the company in alignment with your personal values and ethics? Will this position allow you to use your current strengths while providing growth potential? No one wants a job where they just *show up*—everyone wants to shine and have the chance to grow!

A major key to shining in interviews is to create the language that will best describe you and your skills to a prospective employer. The key to communicating self-awareness is to share this knowledge naturally and make it part of your common vernacular; otherwise, if it feels forced, it may come across as bragging. You want to sound confident, not cocky.

A natural way to communicate self-awareness is to preface a sentence with statement such as, "What I've learned about myself is..." or, "In my experience, what I've found works well (or doesn't work well) is..." Again, this helps by communicating specific examples while displaying a level of self-knowledge and confidence.

Assess your whole interview experience, from entering the parking lot to leaving the building. Be aware of the physical environment, interactions between people, and the "vibes" you get while you're there. This experience is a time to gather more information about this potential workplace starting from the moment you arrive.

Andy was ready for his interview. As he pulled into the parking lot, he took note of the entrance to the building, the grounds, and the sculptures located out front. *The grounds are very nice and well-maintained*, he thought. As he entered the building, he noticed the interior decor, colors, simplicity, and cleanliness of the lobby. The receptionist greeted Andy with a smile and asked him to wait in the seating area.

Andy sat patiently and leafed casually though a magazine. He took several deep breaths, each time releasing any nervousness he was feeling, and reminded himself that this interview was nothing to worry about. *This doesn't need to be a big deal; just treat it as another friendly meeting.*

Andy took note of the people walking around in the office. They all appeared to be in cheerful spirits. The environment felt organized, clean, and healthy. These first impressions were all very important clues that helped Andy to evaluate this potential workplace.

The interview itself is the moment of truth. When you are answering questions during an interview, try to align your answers to specific attributes or skills listed in the job description. This will assist the interviewer in seeing that your skills and talents match the requirements of the position.

Another imperative aspect of interviewing is to demonstrate honesty and integrity. In our personal relationships, this is referred to as vulnerability; in business relationships, it's called *transparency*. With the increasing speed of business in today's economy, transparency isn't just desirable—it's **essential**.

During the interview, Andy paid close attention to the interviewer's body language, tone of voice, and line of questioning. The interviewer also engaged Andy in small talk to put him at ease, but he kept it to a minimum.

The interview seemed to flow well and Andy felt confident and clear about his answers to the interviewer's questions. Andy also felt good about the stories and examples he used for support, as he had been gathering excellent examples during his interview preparation. Andy had gained a lot of clarity by creating his PPG spreadsheet and was prepared to speak about his preferences clearly and calmly during the interview. He noticed that the interviewer often nodded in agreement. This made Andy feel that they were making a good connection.

At the end of the interview, Andy asked a series of questions he had prepared. Then he asked about the next steps and timeline. Andy was told that he was a very strong candidate for the position and that they would be following up with him next week. This was great news and Andy was excited that the interview had gone well.

REALITY CHECK

- People *want* to hire you!
- Interviews are about *alignment.* Remember that you are also **interviewing them**.
- When you have practiced how to speak naturally about you and your experiences, it will be much easier to be transparent and authentic during an interview.

QUESTIONS TO CONSIDER

1) Which interview questions am I most prepared for? Most unprepared for?

2) How can my PPG spreadsheet provide me with more clarity about what I want?

INNER AFFIRMATIONS

"I have the information, language, and courage to interview with calm confidence. I have the ability to activate my thoughts, feelings, and intuition to help me decide whether an environment, working relationship, and organization aligns with me and who I am. I am able to see an interview as a conversation about mutual alignment and a chance to tell someone who I am and what I do."

See *Appendix E: Interviewing Tip Sheet*

CHAPTER 19 — NAVIGATING STORMY SEAS

I am not afraid of storms
for I am learning how to sail my ship.
— Louisa May Alcott

No matter how carefully you assess your strengths, check your alignment, and activate your search, chances are that you'll face some further challenges. We all experience thunderstorms of contrast and winds of adversity, and our boats will be tested. But if we lose the way, we can always return to the guidance that's already within us. That is where our true centers are located, and we can trust that we are always heading in the right direction regardless of our present circumstances.

If we look to science, our brains are actually programmed to be doubtful more than optimistic. In his book, *The Mindful Path to Self-Compassion*, Dr. Christopher Germer tells us, "We have evolved for survival, not happiness, and thus have a natural tendency to focus on the negative." Considering that our brains are naturally hardwired for problem solving, being skeptical comes naturally—call it *pragmatic contingency planning*.

Perhaps you experienced it when friends or loved ones faced a layoff, and you thought about what you'd do if your job was cut. Wondering "What if?" helps us be ready when change comes. It's a healthy response...until doubt and pessimism become your predominant perspective. Then you may need to re-examine your viewpoint.

Problems are simply challenges and present opportunities for creative solutions. In fact, if we didn't have problems, we wouldn't grow. Challenges give us perspective, forcing us to take a step back, reconsider our options, and see things differently. Even though our problems can bring frustration and fear, they can also remind us to stay present and develop patience for the process. Problems allow us to learn from our experiences and remember that behind every storm there is calm.

Focusing attention on fear and doubt will only sabotage our efforts to stay in alignment with our vision and continue moving forward. Adopting an attitude of hope can create a whole new set of possibilities and help to course-correct our direction. Hope is fueled by patience and the confidence that comes from knowing that at all times we have the power to choose which direction we are headed according to what we choose to focus on. **Be patient and confident that you can weather the challenges as you search for a new career direction.**

I was reminded of the impact of doubt recently during a coaching session. My client, Rachel, and I were working on aligning her towards her ideal job. I was asking her a list of standard questions about her job search and what types of work she might be interested in pursuing next.

As we continued our conversation, I noticed a pattern to her responses. Rachel kept saying, "but I can't do (this) or (that)" or "they won't hire me because..." or "I heard there's nothing out there right now in that area..." As our session progressed I watched her doubts grow bigger and bigger.

I gradually saw Rachel using her doubt to:

- Protect her belief systems
- Avoid disappointment
- Bypass fears of re-occurrence
- Confirm her beliefs that finding work was difficult, disappointing, and nearly impossible

I was not surprised: I've heard many people express these same doubts in previous coaching sessions, but I also knew that doubts could be overcome with some simple reminders. The solution is not to eliminate doubt, but rather use doubt to uncover judgments, assumptions, and false beliefs that are no longer valid. This allows us to "upgrade" old beliefs into new understandings.

I gently reminded Rachel to listen to her doubts, release the need to control outcomes, seek to change her perspective to optimistic. Basically, do what you can and then it let go. Rachel took a deep breath, looked at me, and said, "You think I can do that?" to which I promptly replied, "Absolutely."

Rachel had just learned that expressing her doubts were opportunities to remain aware, seek alignment, and trust the process.

REALITY CHECK

- Our brains are programmed for problem solving and survival, not happiness.
- You have the ability to overcome your doubts and fears.
- Our doubts and fears give us important information about our current belief systems.

QUESTIONS TO CONSIDER

1) In what ways might my doubts and fears teaching me more about myself?

2) How can I learn from my problems? What can they teach me?

INNER AFFIRMATIONS

"I realize that my problems and challenges are merely opportunities in disguise. They provide more chances for me to know myself as I am. I am learning patience, perseverance, and how to choose my thoughts wisely. I believe that I can replace my doubts and fears with hope and confidence."

See *Appendix F: Your Mind: Creature, Teacher, or Companion?*

CHAPTER 20 — MAKING LEMONADE

> *It's as good as it can be for how bad it is.*
> — Tom Sunnarborg, after our family home
> was destroyed by fire in 2002

Thoughts are extremely powerful. In fact, our thoughts create reality as we experience it. Much like setting GPS coordinates when navigating a new destination, thoughts will create a roadmap and take us in the direction of our attention. So, in which direction are you headed?

Within each of us is an "emotional default setting" that is formed by the environments and the people around us during our impressionable childhood years. Over years of repetition, this default setting became the foundation for a set of matching beliefs and chronic patterns of thought associated with those beliefs. Thoughts are productive when they're positive, but negative thoughts block progress. **Negative thoughts create** *limiting beliefs.*

Limiting beliefs may include statements such as:

- "I have no choice."
- "Other people always seem so much happier than me."
- "I always get the raw end of the deal."

Each of these statements has come from limiting beliefs. However, many of these beliefs are created by simple observations—for example, a single experience or observation—or they have been passed down to us by others (for example, parents or friends) and we've chosen to believe them.

Especially after a layoff or career transition, our thoughts have the potential to immobilize us. By being aware of our limiting beliefs, we can start to create a new set of affirmations that will help us, and not keep hurting us.

A different perspective that can quickly bring hope, clarity, and relief is known as *reframing*. Reframing is the practice of recognizing that **how we respond** to something is just as important—if not more important—than our initial reaction. By recognizing that we are in control of our responses, then life changes, including job transitions, are opportunities to redefine and recreate ourselves.

Reframing always gives us options, especially with limiting beliefs:

- "I have no choice" becomes *"I always have choices, even if it's only my attitude."*
- "Other people always seem so much happier than I am" becomes *"I realize that I am responsible for my own happiness, and other happy people inspire me."*
- "I always get the raw end of the deal" becomes *"I know that my attitude is everything, and I am responsible for choosing the best perspective I can about my life."*

Reframing is based in accepting reality as it is while embracing an attitude of optimism. It is the skill that can move us into the next chapter of our lives. Reframing includes developing a higher tolerance for ambiguity—the ability to be comfortable with unknown variables—and being open to taking a new perspective without requiring proof to back it up. **Reframing requires trust and facilitates hope.**

It was apparent at an early age that I was gifted with an "abundance of energy." During my first years of elementary school, my teachers enjoyed my creativity and enthusiasm. However, my third grade teacher found my gregarious nature to be a bit challenging—so she tried something different.

When my Mom and Dad came to the parent/teacher conferences that fall, they walked around the classroom looking for my desk. "Where's Mike's desk?" my Dad asked. "Oh," said the teacher, "I put his desk back there," pointing to the back of the room.

My parents walked back to find that my desk had been placed behind a folding screen. As they looked at my space, they smiled to each other. I had decorated the whole inside of the screen with pictures of rainbows, smiling faces, and other colorful drawings. There was even a sign hanging up that read, *Mike's Place.*

Initially confused by this placement, my resilient creative spirit had decided to make the best of the situation. Instead of this being an obstacle, it became an opportunity. I had created my own office. And who wouldn't love that?!

My Mom and Dad waited along with the other parents for their turn to speak with my teacher. During their conference, they learned that her plan to isolate my enthusiasm had backfired. Seeing what I created had prompted the other kids to ask, "When do we get *our turn* in the back?"

Upon hearing the teacher's explanation, my Dad turned to my Mom and said, "Just a chip off the old block," to which my Mom nodded in agreement. Spontaneous creativity runs in our family.

Now when life hands me lemons, I go back to my third grade office and remind myself that I have the power to respond to a potentially negative experience and reframe it into a positive one. I can step into any situation and have the confidence and assurance that things will eventually work out for the best.

I've learned to make lemonade.

REALITY CHECK

- Being aware of our limiting beliefs can allow us to transform them.
- Reframing gives us more options.
- There is learning in every experience.

QUESTIONS TO CONSIDER

1) How can reframing my attitude affect the outcome of my career transition?

2) In what ways am I making lemonade out of the lemons of this experience?

INNER AFFIRMATIONS

"I have the ability to reframe my perspective about anything: a circumstance, event, person, or action. I know that I will directly experience a result from the attitude that I choose, and that attitude will affect my actions and words. Therefore, I can think very carefully about how I choose to respond to this and any other life challenge."

CHAPTER 21 — LIFE IS THE JOURNEY

What is the meaning of life? Whatever you want it to be.
— James Frey

For many people, the search for the meaning of life is an ongoing quest without an answer; others can find meaning and purpose in every moment.

Some believe that life's meaning and purpose will arrive when they finally *get there*. So what is "there"? The definition will be different for everyone. There might be a new job, finding your soul mate, or buying your first house—it really depends on your intentions and expectations.

The reality is that we never actually get there since the only place we can physically be is *here* in the present moment. And although our powerful thoughts and imagination can take us in many directions—into the past or future—the present moment is where all of our power is. The moment we have right now is our moment of creation, and *we are the creators of our own reality.* Everything else is simply memory or imagination.

Your challenge is to be content in the present moment and learn to be here. And then when you finally get that new job, relationship, or life experience, you can appreciate what you've learned along the way. This perspective can remind us that life is, indeed, about appreciating the whole journey—"here"—and not just the destination—"there."

Is life perfect? Absolutely not. But **our lives were never meant to be perfect; they were meant to be purposeful.** We can derive an incredible amount of happiness and joy from our greatest experiences while at the same time realizing that from our most challenging times can come powerful moments of renewed meaning and clarity.

We are all going about our lives day-to-day and navigating through the seas of life, which bring waves, lulls, and uncharted waters. We all have good days; we all have challenging days. Sometimes we're right on course; sometimes we're headed for an iceberg. Other times, we just need to take our eyes off the map for a moment and allow the winds of change to take us in a new direction. Either way, the voyage continues.

> After calling my parents the morning I was laid off, I decided to go home and spend the weekend with them. They only lived a few hours away. And since they were two of my best friends, there was nobody I'd rather see that day. So I drove home.
>
> That weekend, I began sifting through the gamut of my feelings: shock, anger, denial, and disappointment—basically, the grieving process had begun for me. As a writer, I did what comes naturally whenever I start processing: I wrote down my feelings. Or as one of my favorite authors, Julia Cameron, says, "Put it on the page."

One morning, I visualized a blog post called *The White Box Club*. Later, as I went back to my notes, I started to see book chapters forming. It was then that I got the nudge. I knew that this powerful event was another opportunity to share with others and validate their experience—to write another book. It just felt like the right thing to do.

I wrote the initial blog post and began assembling the chapters during subsequent weeks. I wanted to share the experience in real time in order to embrace it fully. I chose to go with the flow and see where it would lead me. It has lead me here.

REALITY CHECK

- We are the creators of our own realities.
- We can learn to be content in the present moment, the now.
- Our most powerful moments can come from our most challenging experiences.

QUESTIONS TO CONSIDER

1) How can I learn to appreciate the experiences that my life journey has given me?

2) What do I believe is ahead for me in the future?

INNER AFFIRMATIONS

"I know that the present moment is my moment of creation. I embrace my life experience knowing that it is an ongoing process, and I am receiving all of the lessons that my life experiences are bringing to me. I am always learning and growing, and all is well."

CLOSING

Sometimes I've believed as many as
six impossible things before breakfast.
— Lewis Carroll

Now that you've read each of the chapters, answered the questions, and completed the exercises, I encourage you to apply what you've learned to help create a smooth and successful career transition. As you move into this new chapter of your life, consider what your career has taught you about yourself, your strengths, and what fulfills your sense of purpose. Remember: Only you can decide how to respond to the challenges that life gives you. It's always your choice.

My hope is that you will see yourself as a person worthy of a joyous, fulfilling, and abundant career. That you can *do what you love* and *love what you do,* and that your gifts and talents will be shared and appreciated by others. Once you realize that life is truly about the adventure of creating yourself, you will be able respond to the transitions of life more objectively—regardless of the circumstances.

I believe in you, and I believe you can make anything happen. Focus on what you truly desire. Be brave. Be bold. Savor the moments and memories with those around you. Live life to its fullest and believe that your life has meaning and purpose. Because it does.

APPENDIX
EXERCISE SUPPLEMENTS

Appendix A — Financial Assessment Checklist

Bills, Payments, Accounts

Name	Type	Amount	Frequency	Notes
(e.g. U.S. Bank)	(e.g. Credit card)	450.78	Monthly	(e.g. Travel account)
...				

Lifestyle Expenses

Name	Type	Amount	Frequency	Notes
(e.g. Anytime Fitness)	(e.g. Gym membership)	52	Monthly	(e.g. auto pay)
...				

Other Expenses

Daily Expenses				
Food				
...				

APPENDIX B — PERSONAL PRIORITY GRID (PPG)

First, think about the type of career details you'd like to create in your next experience:

- Environment: location, size, physical space, proximity, workplace culture
- People: personalities, behaviors, values, "vibes"
- Organizational Values: mission, vision, purpose, direction, product or service
- Commitment to developing YOU: using your talents, growing your skills, investing in your career path

Now create the Personal Priority Grid to help you to get very clear about the things you really want and don't want, and what you're willing to accept in a new career opportunity. Take a piece of paper, make three columns, add the words shown below in boldface to each column header and fill in information that pertains to you (based on your past experience) below each heading like this:

Don't Want	Willing to Accept	Do Want
M-F 8-5 with no flexibility	Work from home 2 x week	Flexible hours
Micromanaging or controlling boss	Boss who is reasonably supportive	Supportive leader/boss
Unclear objectives, undefined work or timelines	Reasonably clear objectives, time is determined and fixed	Clear objectives, long leash
...	...	...

This simple exercise will help you quickly **prioritize** what you want and why. It will also help you during the interviewing process when you are faced with these types of questions: i.e., "What kind of work do you enjoy? What kind of leadership works best for you? What type of work schedule do you prefer? In what type of work environment do you work best?"

In addition, the more you work on your PPG, the more you will start to **form the language** for what you really want to create next.

Here's an example:

- Lauren started to list what she *didn't want* in the first column; for example: 1) typical 8-5 business hours; 2) a micromanaging boss; and 3) unclear expectations.
- Then in the far right column, she listed one-for-one what she *did want* as opposed to the things she didn't want; for example: 1) flexible hours and work schedule; 2) a leader who empowered her; and 3) clear expectations.
- In the middle column, Lauren wrote what she was *willing to accept* between the two extremes—her "negotiation ground"; for example: 1) a day or two working from home, if traditional business hours were desired; 2) a boss willing to learn and be flexible about their leadership style; and 3) some clear expectations, but some free-flowing goals.

With this knowledge and clarity, Lauren will be able to speak clearly about her personal preferences and priorities to friends, colleagues, and (especially) potential employers!

Appendix C — Resume Tip Sheet

- Find your words/language, keywords.
- Who are you? Create a bio or bullet list.
- What value will you bring to the employer/job?
- Focus on your past accomplishments and achievements, not your responsibilities.
- What are your exceptional qualities? What sets you apart?
- Everything skill is transferrable – be creative!
- State the facts and be clear (use numbers, percentages and statistics when possible).
- Start with verbs; keep descriptions to 10 words or less.
- Don't lie, but don't downplay either.
- Make your resume into conversation points.
- Be careful about what you put out on social media (be mindful of recruiters and potential employers).
- Resume = report of what it is you want them to know about your career path; use past tense verbs—no need for OBJECTIVE (use Summary instead). You want them to know about at least 10 years' experience. Have multiple resumes (at least two to three with the same main content). No more than five lines of text, six bullets maximum. Put your power up-front (a computer reads first 120 words); specific keywords; write for humans; create a resume with two pages, front-side only.
- Summary = help them know what it is you want (PPG); don't make them be detectives. The first line is your BRAND.
- Cover letter = why you're interested in **them,** and their company (do your homework!). An explanation of WHY—values, reasons. First paragraph: what you LIKE about them, learned about them (care, motivation). Second paragraph: What do you bring? Third paragraph: Action, follow-up, name, phone number.

Appendix D — Networking Tip Sheet

Helpful Tips for Natural Networkers:

- Surround yourself with people who support you—people whom you enjoy!
- Strengthen your existing network by making more connections. Ask to be introduced to more people and seek to find common ground in each new relationship that you develop.
- Keep contact information updated—yours and those in your network. Alert people when you change your contact information and be sure to keep your contacts current. Make it as easy for them to find you as it is for you to find them.
- Continue to grow and develop your network along with your own personal growth and development. Reach out to your network and let them support you. Think of your network as your own personal cheering section!
- Get CLEAR on what you want and what language you need to use to support speaking to it.
- ASK to meet new people.

Helpful Tips for New Networkers:

- Try attending more events in which you are forced to meet new people. Make a point to meet at least three new people at every event or function that you attend.
- When you meet someone for the first time, exchange business cards or contact information and send them a thank you note as soon as possible. This is not only a polite gesture, but it establishes a more permanent way

to contact each other (i.e. Outlook, address book, contact list).

- Stay connected to your Connectors! They will remain a valuable resource for you as you build and expand your own personal network.

- Networking is about relationships and helping others. It's about people. It's about connection. It's about authenticity and transparency. It's about maintenance and upkeep.

Appendix E — Interviewing Tip Sheet

- Who are you?
- What will you bring to the employer/job?
- Never underestimate the value of stories.
- Don't lie, but don't downplay either.
- Go with your gut on how much you say/don't say.
- Keep it simple, avoid "over sharing."
- Know your priorities. What are your deal breakers? (Remember your PPG Grid?)
- Know thyself. Be able to tell people what works for you (i.e., In my experience, I've found that I work best...").
- Tune into the "vibe"—life is too short to work with people whom you don't like.
- Give them a reason to remember you, but not too big a reason.
- Don't be afraid to ask for what you want ("I'd like to work remotely two days a week...") even if they don't offer it as part of the package – you never get what you don't ask for!
- Be willing to negotiate; be flexible but firm.

Tips from Recruiters:

- Headhunters are independent and hired to help you find work for a fee.
- Recruiters work for the company so you don't pay a fee. Recruiters generally look at resumes in the following way: first scan = 6 seconds (looking for keywords, skills, visual); second scan: take more time, looking at details.

- If you get a phone screening, that is good! This generally means they want to interview you and probably hire you. Now they are looking for red flags or reasons to screen you out vs. other candidates.

- Be transparent during the interview: were you laid off? Fired? Why? Did you have lag time? Transition? It's okay! Be honest if they ask.

- Recruiters are not looking at just responsibilities, but accomplishments (like on your resume).

- During the interview, tell your stories, but be brief. What did you learn? How has your experience changed you into the person you are today? Draw connections.

- Focus on your strengths.

- Recruiters and hiring managers ask "behavior-based" questions based on the theory that future performance is based on past performance.

- The workplace has more agility now. 2+ years in any position is sufficient.

- Salaries: look on Salary.com by geographical area for ranges.

- If an interviewer asks you about your salary history, ask them, "What is the range for this role?" NEVER give anyone your salary history or last salary amount unless it's required, for some reason.

- Be BOLD when answering questions and providing information. YOU decide *what* to share and *how much*.

- Let the interviewer start "small talk." That generally means they like you. Feel free to respond, but keep it simple and brief.

- USE YOUR NETWORK. Ask people about the company and position you are applying for. Ask questions like, "Can you tell me more about the role? Company? What do you know about the position? Do you know someone you can give my resume to?"

- Whenever you're going to use your networking contacts to help connect to the hiring manager or recruiter, always apply also online for the job and get into their company system.

- Ask about the company! Ask about the role! Be INTERESTED.

- At the end of the interview, ask about next steps: "What happens next? When?" Ask them about their decision timeline.

- If the interviewer tells you more about the interviewing process and when you should be hearing back from them (i.e., "We are interviewing other candidates this week and will follow-up with you next week...") that is usually a good sign. If they're reluctant to provide follow-up information, it may be your clue that the interview didn't go well. Don't worry—there are plenty of other opportunities waiting for you!

- Always send a thank-you note or email.

APPENDIX F — YOUR MIND: TEACHER, CREATURE, OR COMPANION

"It's mind over matter." "Make up your mind!" "Oh, never mind..." Just think about how frequently the word "mind" enters our daily conversations. Our minds are an integral part of our three-part being: mind, body, and spirit. We often associate the mind with our head, thought, and logic. But despite the *form* that we imagine our minds to take, there are some very different *roles* the mind can play in our daily lives:

Teacher: The mind is a powerful and complex teacher. It "re-minds" us when we've forgotten facts or figures and helps us through a challenging problem. It causes us to stop and think when we need to make a decision and uses our previous experiences as reference in order to make better choices. It keeps a record of everything we've ever thought, said, and done and uses memory to bring us the gift of contrast.

Our mind works with our feelings and sends us signals that something might be awry and we need to pay attention to it. It is the reflective and supportive advisor—helping us weigh the pros and cons from changing our Internet service provider to changing our views about the importance of diet and exercise. It's with us every day, every hour, every minute and doesn't like to be shut off. But once in a while it will allow us to be away from it... maybe for a minute or an hour...and then when we reunite it's like plugging back in and booting up the computer. Class is back in session.

Creature: The mind is a powerful and complex creature. It creeps around and waits for the opportunity to jump out and scare us, or catches us by surprise when we're not looking. It lurks around the dark corners with a mirror and attempts to make us look into it and judge our appearance. It can be the constant critic, judge, and antagonist, carrying around a thick history book of everything we've ever thought, said, and done and then re-minds us about our mistakes and uses them against us like a court of law where we're guilty until proven innocent.

Our mind has a voice recorder that plays back every negative word that every person has said to us, sticking to our fears like a sliver we can't remove. It keeps us up worrying at night, wakes us up with a headache in the morning, and never stops running. And we're tired of the chase. Sometimes we'd rather be without it. It makes us conform when we've been scolded and makes us feel ashamed for who we are. It can be our worst enemy. And if we spend too much time focusing on what it is constantly saying, it can make us feel crazy and out of control.

Companion: The mind is a powerful and complex companion. It wishes us happy birthday and re-minds us where we parked the car in the stadium parking lot. It's there to provide a history of everything we've ever thought, said, and done, and then uses our success to re-mind us about how far we've come. It plays back the recordings of anyone who's ever thanked us, praised us, or shouted our name as we raced toward the finish line. It allows us to take a moment to pause and reflect upon a fond memory triggered by a beautiful song or the smell of fresh-baked cookies.

Our mind is there to help us stay calm amidst a crisis or speak a kind word to a friend in need. It's our constant friend, confidant, and partner. And it always answers when we call. It's there to motivate, encourage, and inspire us and becomes the coach urging us to hang in there and "just keep swimming." It reminds us that it's okay to make mistakes and it forgives us our mistakes every time—no exception. It loves and accepts us as we are. It is our best friend and our family. It holds us when we are alone and reminds us that everything will be okay.

Question: Is your mind playing the role of teacher, creature, or companion today? Depending on the situation, it could be playing the role of one, two, or all three at once. But the most important thing to remember is that it's *our choice* to pay attention to what feels best. Whichever voice we focus on becomes the loudest.

The best part is that we can control our minds. We can choose to focus on the teacher, creature, or the companion. When our minds are working *for* us in a positive and supportive way, we can better connect with our inner beings and bring alignment and consistency to our lives.

This article originally featured as a blog post on: michaelsunnarborg.com/blog

ABOUT THE AUTHOR

Michael Thomas Sunnarborg is a professional speaker, best-selling author, and life transition coach. He's spent his life living in different parts of the world including Europe, Asia, and the South Pacific. To stimulate his creative flow, Michael is also a professional photographer for which he has won several awards. In addition to his line of best-selling books, Michael's blogs and photo galleries have been followed by thousands of readers worldwide, including photos licensed and sold by National Geographic. Michael currently lives in Minneapolis, Minnesota.

For information on coaching, presentations, workshops and other books by Michael Thomas Sunnarborg, visit michaelsunnarborg.com

OTHER BOOKS BY
MICHAEL THOMAS SUNNARBORG

*Balancing Work, Relationships
& Life in Three Simple Steps*

*21 Keys to Work/Life Balance:
Unlock Your Full Potential*

*21 Steps to Better Relationships:
Find More Balance with Others*

*21 Days to Better Balance:
Find More Balance in a Busy World*

Inspiration from the World

Order additional copies of this book and eBook at:
michaelsunnarborg.com / books

Follow on social media at:

Twitter: @21daystobalance

Facebook: 21daystobetterbalance

LinkedIn: michaelthomassunnarborg

ACKNOWLEDGEMENTS

This book would not have been possible
without the help of some very special people.

A very special thank you to:
Tom & Yvonne Sunnarborg, and Kiernon James

Love and support from:
Becky, Jim, Nicolette & Natalie Wontor,
Dorothy Navarro, Shawn Boyd, Jay Schoenfeld,
Mary Texer, Peggy Foster, and Chad Tearle

Inspiration from:
Kathleen & Scott Blanc, Sheila Feigin, Ann E. Boyum,
Laura Ventrella, Jerry & Esther Hicks and Abraham, the
music of Altus and Lisa Gerrard

Friendship from:
Robert Holloway & Aaron Gilbert, Kathy Messerli,
Rob Reitz, Joshua Avery, JoAnn Van Sloun, Amy Smith,
Susan Hawkins, Eric Gross, Laurie, Sharon Fleming,
Wendy Griak, Rod Johnson, Kevin Loo

My favorite writing spaces:
The CW Loft, CW West & CW North Pole,
Caribou Coffee, Delta Airlines, and Blytheville

Silence and solitude compliments of:
The White Falcon

Be Well.

46527010R00079

Made in the USA
Lexington, KY
07 November 2015